AuthorHouse™ LLC
1663 Liberty Drive
Bloomington, IN 47403
www.authorhouse.com
Phone: 1-800-839-8640

© 2014 Patricia Palermo. All rights reserved.

No part of this book may be reproduced, stored in a retrieval system,
or transmitted by any means without the written permission of the author.

Published by AuthorHouse 01/29/2014

ISBN: 978-1-4918-5823-3 (sc)
ISBN: 978-1-4918-5822-6 (e)

Library of Congress Control Number: 2014901820

Any people depicted in stock imagery provided by Thinkstock are models,
and such images are being used for illustrative purposes only.
Certain stock imagery © Thinkstock.

This book is printed on acid-free paper.

Because of the dynamic nature of the Internet, any web addresses or links contained in this book may have changed since publication and may no longer be valid. The views expressed in this work are solely those of the author and do not necessarily reflect the views of the publisher, and the publisher hereby disclaims any responsibility for them.

The Best Gift I Have Is You

I would like to dedicate this book to my husband Frank,

my three children, Adelina, Alessandro and Victoria.

You are truly the best gift I have been blessed with.

Mommy, what do you want for your birthday?

I will pick you the most beautiful flowers from the garden.

I will make you the biggest card.

I will bake you the sweetest cake.

I will work very hard!

All I want for my birthday is you!

Mommy, what do you want for Christmas?

I will buy you the prettiest dress.

I will buy you the shiniest ring.

I will give you my favorite toy.

And I will dance, play music and sing.

All I want for Christmas is you!

Mommy, what do you want for Valentine's Day?

I will cut out a large cupid

holding a red heart above.

I will write you a long letter

filled with stories about love.

All I want for Valentine's Day is you!

Mommy, what do you want for Easter?

I will paint you the most colorful eggs.

I will buy you the biggest chocolate bunny.

I will fill up a basket with goodies.

And have them delivered to you. Won't that be funny?

All I want for Easter is you!

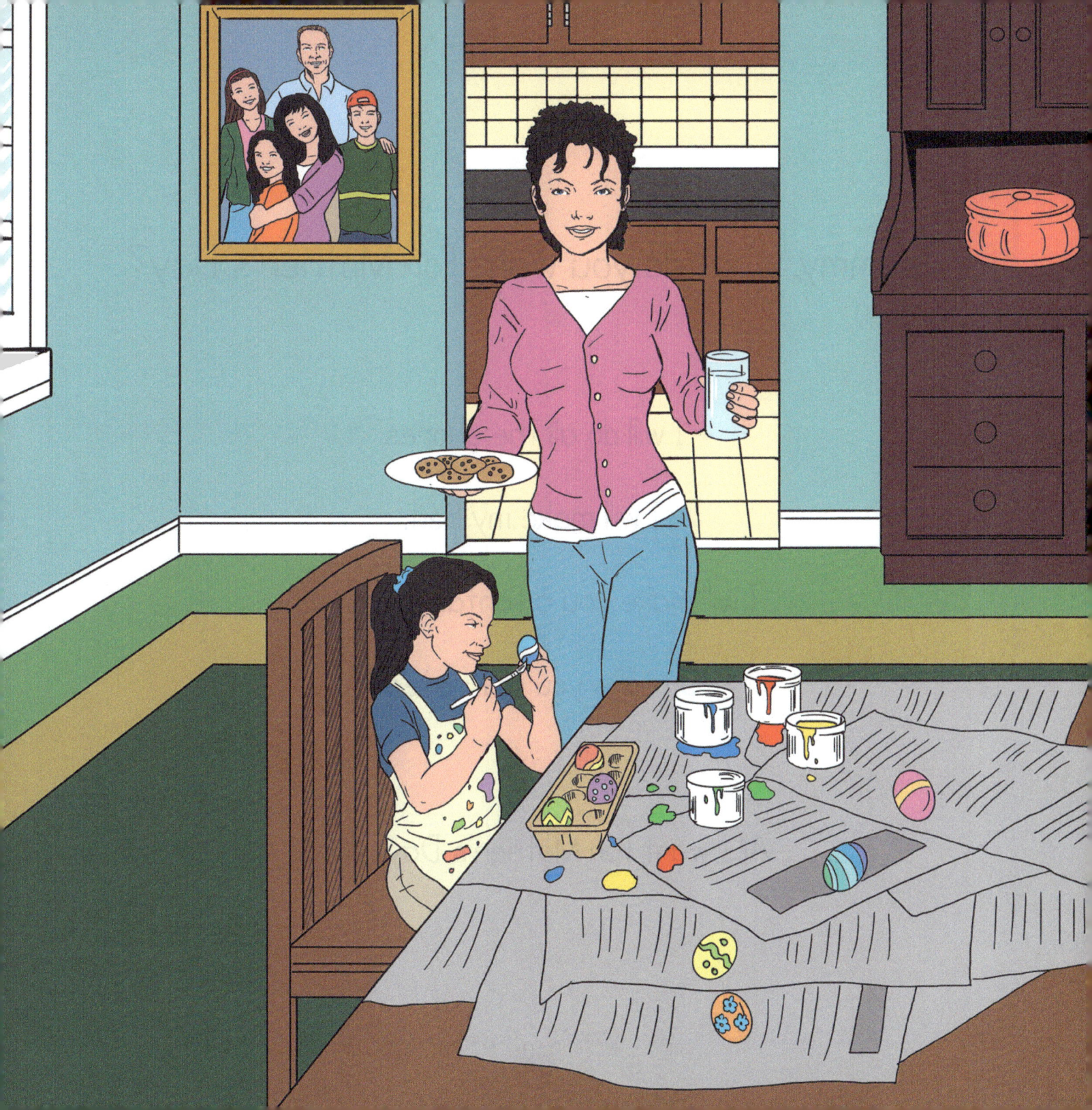

Mommy, what do you want for Mother's Day?

I will do all the chores.

I will make my bed.

I will make you a fantastic dinner.

Or take you out instead.

All I want for Mother's Day is you!

You are so special to me.

I could not have asked for anything more.

You are the **best gift I have.**

You are better than any gift from a store.

I appreciate all the things you want to make for me.

But the one thing I want is you in my life,

which makes me so happy.

CPSIA information can be obtained at www.ICGtesting.com
Printed in the USA
LVOW02s2046070214

372842LV00001B/1/P

9 781491 858233